Holly
Three White Mice

written by Corinne Fenton

illustrated by Jacqueline East

Holly loved mice.
She loved black mice, brown mice and grey mice.

But most of all,
Holly loved her three pet white mice.
They all lived in a special box
in her bedroom.

Every summer, Holly and her family went on an overnight fishing trip. But this summer, Holly didn't want to go. She wanted to stay home with her three white mice.

"Mrs Brooks will take care of your mice," said Dad, smiling at Holly.
"She will come over this afternoon and feed them for you."

Holly turned sadly to her three white mice.
"You must be very good while I'm away," she whispered.
"You must stay in your box
and wait quietly for me to come home."

But Holly's mice didn't wait quietly at all.
As soon as Holly had gone,
they ran up the side of their box
and pushed their way through a tiny hole
in the corner.
It was very easy!

Holly's three white mice had a lovely time
running all over the house.
They ran in and out of the bedrooms
and up and down the stairs.
They even ran into the kitchen
to look for something to eat.

That afternoon, when Mrs Brooks found
their empty box, she was **very** upset.
She looked all over the house
for Holly's three white mice,
but she couldn't find them anywhere.

When Holly arrived home the next day,
Mrs Brooks came running over.
"I'm **so** sorry," she said.
"Your three white mice
got out of their box and ran away.
I've looked all over the house,
but I can't find them."

A small tear ran down Holly's cheek.

9

"Oh, dear!" cried Mum,
as she walked into the kitchen.
"What a terrible mess!"
The bench was covered in flour,
and so was the floor.
Flour was everywhere!

"I wonder who did this,"
said Dad, looking around.

"I have no idea," said Mum.

But Holly had an idea.
She picked up the box of flour.
There, in the corner, was a big hole.

"Oh!" cried Holly, turning towards
Mum and Dad.
"I'm **so** sorry.
My naughty white mice have been here."

"Yes," said Mum sadly,
"and we need to find them
before they get into more things."

"Look!" said Holly.
"I can see some tiny white footprints
going down the hall.
If we follow them, we might find
my naughty white mice."

13

So Mum, Dad and Holly followed the tiny white footprints. They went down the hall and into Holly's bedroom.

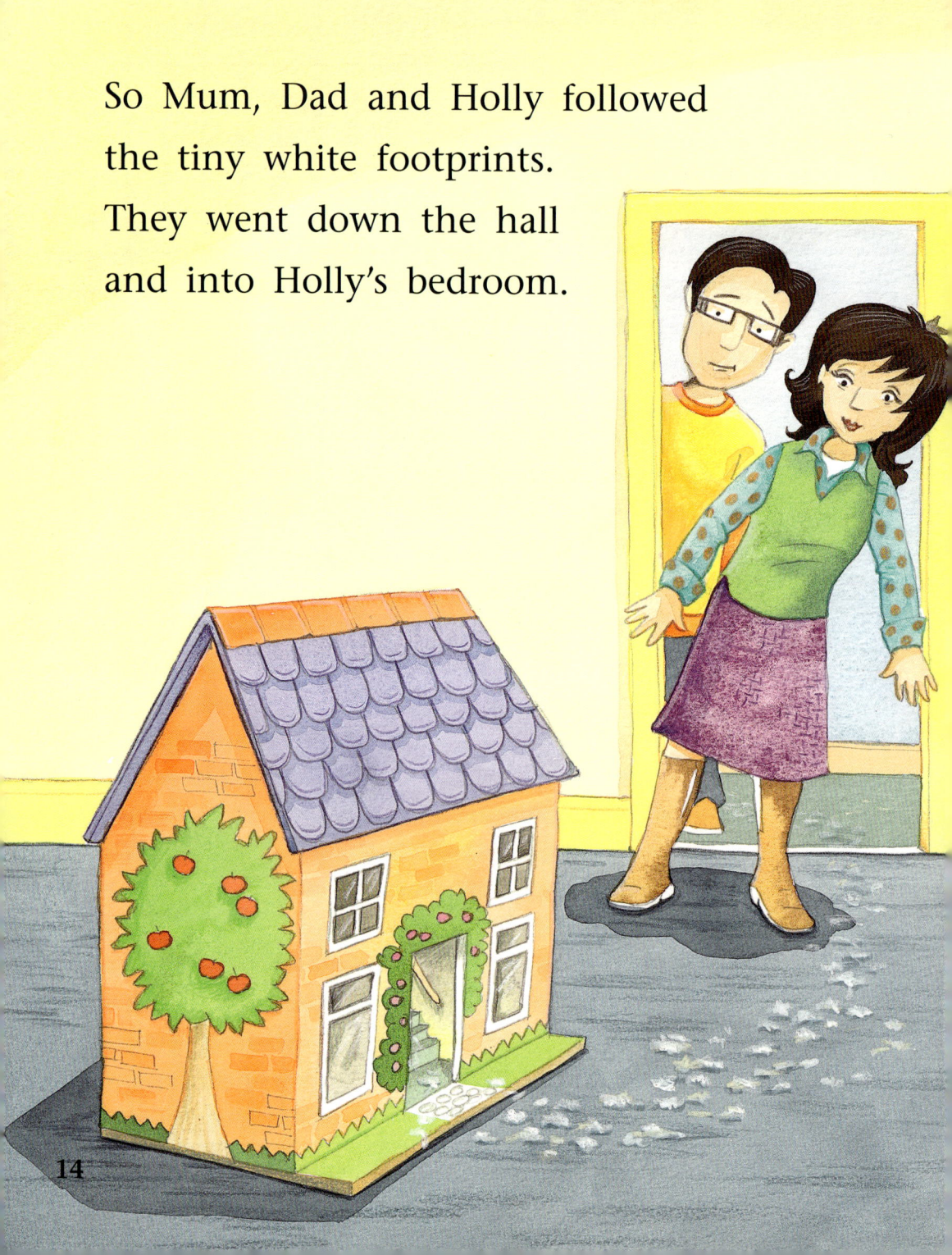

"Look!" said Holly.
"The footprints go into my doll's house."
Three sets of tiny footprints went
through the door, up the stairs
and into the bedroom.
Holly got down on her knees
and peeked through the window.

And there, fast asleep,
were her naughty white mice.
"Oh," whispered Holly,
"you are very naughty little mice,
but I'm so glad to see you!"

Holly's sleepy white mice just opened
their eyes and blinked.